Arbor Wordsworth
July 8

GW00693967

Brain Nutrients

Sharpen Your Mind, Prevent Alzheimer's Disease

KATE GILBERT UDALL

WOODLAND PUBLISHING
Pleasant Grove, Utah

[Handwritten left column:]

cfw
1. "headstand" — rest
   on head/ slant-board/
   blood to brain

2. Essential oils for brain
   massage into scalp.

3. lecithin

4. Exercise ⚡
   (lots of nutrients, but
   if circulation + O₂ aren't
   reaching brain, won't make
   use of them.)

5. Breaths

6. Mineral rehydration

7. Coconut oil — Omega 3s

8. Cod — liver cleanse

9. Clay absorbs
   toxins
   radio active stuff

10. Inflammation — Turmeric

11. Growth hormone & Melatonin.

[Handwritten right column:]

this Book
Scientific evidence
p6. Vit E
    DHA
    Alpha Lipoic Acid
    Ginseng
    Ginko Biloba
    Huperzine A

p6 anti-oxidants
 • (barefoot on earth — the
    electrons)
 • Clay. absorbs + charged

12. Foods w Vit E & Ginko
                 Biloba
13. Ginseng ⚡
14. Inflammation curcumin
         turmeric
15. Huperzine A
16. Alpha Lipoic Acid

N.pole magnets — eye mask

Contents

Enhancing Brain Function:
An Introduction

It's not hard for any of us to see how important our brain's activities are in everything we do, and the extent to which our brain functions at an optimal level is central to our success in life. What you may not know is that you can do something to enhance the activity of your brain. Because the tissues of the brain are delicate and susceptible to both positive and negative influences, healthy brain tissue should be a high priority concern.

Research has shown that many nutrients can increase productivity of brain cells as well as help maintain proper function of the brain. They do this by

- protecting against free radicals;
- facilitating neuron development in early brain development;
- decreasing age-related brain cell damage;
- improving memory;

- balancing the body's systems in times of stress;
- and improving circulation to the brain.

Beneficial supplements such as certain antioxidants, essential fatty acids, and natural herbs as well as other compounds can actually reverse some of the symptoms of diseases affecting the brain, like Alzheimer's and Parkinson's disease. Primary agents which have scientific evidence to support their efficacy are:

- Vitamin E
- DHA
- Alpha Lipoic Acid
- Ginseng
- Ginkgo biloba
- Huperzine A

When we understand the biological effects of these nutrients and the mechanisms by which they operate, we can plan for future prevention and treatment of some of the most common neural diseases as well as work towards achievement of optimal brain function. This booklet will be devoted to discussing how these primary agents work to stimulate and facilitate strong brain activity and to review the current supporting research.

About Antioxidants

What's all the commotion about antioxidants? Are they really essential for healthy brain tissue? The answer is a resounding "yes." As the body ages, progressive defects in the protection against free radicals allow an increase in tissue damage and eventually lead to various problems in the brain and other parts of the body. What antioxidants do is to protect brain tissue and other cells from the destruction brought on by age. Antioxidants are necessary, because they fight the effects of free radicals in the body, particularly in the brain.

THE FREE RADICAL CYCLE

Free radicals are molecules with electrons that are unpaired. If a molecule has an electron that does not have a partner, it becomes unstable and reactive. Free radicals steal electrons from other stable molecules in order to become stable themselves. Once the electrons are paired, the molecules becomes stable and nonreactive. When a stable molecule loses an electron to a free radical, it becomes another free radical that will in turn steal an electron from yet another molecule. And so, a destructive cycle begins. Basically, "each time a molecule loses an electron, it is damaged and will damage another molecule" (Lin 11). Radicals do not react with any great selectivity, and the chain reactions they set off are a basic principle of free radical chemistry (Gutteridge 7).

Though damaging to cells, free radicals are formed as a result of normal body functions or the interaction of factors external to the body. As the body uses nutrients and oxygen to create energy, oxygen molecules with unpaired electrons—free radicals—are created. These by-products of normal metabolism cause extensive damage to DNA, protein, and lipids, which is clearly manifest in reduced brain productivity and function. Exposure to radiation, whether from the sun or medical X-rays, and environmental pollutants such as tobacco smoke and car exhaust also contribute to the formation of free radicals.

BENEFITS OF VITAMIN E

Vitamin E is a major antioxidant shown to be of value in deterring disease and maintaining overall health. It is one of the most popular vitamins in America and deserves its popularity. A host of literature shows that higher levels of vitamin E have beneficial effects on overall health. It plays a role in protecting against cancer, degenerative diseases, aging, and toxicity. Vitamin E is a generic name for a group of naturally occurring substances found mainly in plant oils that exhibit vitamin E-like activity. The main substances are various types of tocopherols and an almost identical family of substances called tocotrienols. Alpha-tocopherol is the most common form of vitamin E found in the human diet.

Vitamin E works specifically to fight free radicals in fatty areas, most importantly in the fat cells that make up the membrane around each body cell. Tocopherols (vitamin E) scavenge fat radicals much faster than the radicals that react with nearby fatty acid chains or with membrane proteins. Tocopherols also fight free radicals in the blood (Ibid 53). It is important to supplement your body with additional vitamin E, because as it scavenges radical chains, it is often consumed. Body reactions involving oxygen, although necessary, increase the need for all antioxidants, including vitamin E—the major free radical scavenger in the human body.

Vitamin E also works to prevent aging by prolonging the useful life of cells in the body. As the body ages, progressive defects in the protection against free radicals allow an increase in tissue damage and eventually lead to various problems. It has been shown that the red blood cells of those who take vitamin E supplements age far less that the red blood cells of people who do not take supplements (Leiberman 6). A national study found that vitamin E delays the progression of Alzheimer's disease. Researchers tracked 341 moderately senile patients and fond that those who took 2,000 IU of vitamin E took several months longer to reach an advanced stage of the disease (Sano et al 1217). While antioxidants like vitamin E can help prevent deterioration, other nutrients are necessary for formation and prevention.

Why Essential Fatty Acids are Essential

As awareness of the immense scope of essential fatty acid activity grows, it seems incredible that these substances were overlooked until twenty years ago. Research shows that essential fatty acids, and specifically a certain type of fatty acids—the omega-3 fatty acids, are needed for the structural development of brain and neural tissue. Researchers note that if we can describe the biological effects of omega-3 fatty acids such as DHA and the mechanisms by which they operate, we can initiate an intelligent and appropriate plan for future prevention and treatment of some of the most common diseases in our societies. Deficiencies of DHA and other fatty acids have been linked to mental disorders and problems with the nervous system among others.

EFFECTS OF DHA DEFICIENCY

DHA, an omega-3 fatty acid, has received much attention recently because of its role in brain development. Numerous studies target the effects of DHA deficiencies in the body, particularly in the brain and nervous system. Trials involving monkeys, piglets and rats, fed diets deficient in omega-3 fatty acids show that the animals develop changes in the composition of their neural membranes with a significant decrease in DHA (Neuringer et al 272-73). Symptoms include visual impairment and blurring, reduced levels of DHA in the synaptosomes and retina, impaired learning, and other nervous and vision-related conditions. Conditions include:

SPECIES	EFFECTS Of DHA DEFICIENCY
Chicken	Neural tissue DHA depletion
Rat	Impaired learning
Monkey	Reduced visual acuity

Source: Nettleton, Joyce. "Omega-3 Fatty Acids and Health." (See bibliography for detailed reference.)

BRAIN DEVELOPMENT

When asked whether or not omega-3 fatty acids, and specifically DHA, are important for various body processes, health and science experts now largely answer "yes". One notable application of DHA is its role in the development of the brain and nervous system. How much of the brain is comprised of DHA? The exact portion is not known, but is believed to be at least 30 percent and probably more. DHA is involved in the makeup of synaptosomes and synaptic vesicles (both involved in regulating nerve impulse transmission), myelin (the protective sheaths around certain nerves), and mitochondria (minute rods that serve as centers of cellular respiration and energy production in nearly all of the body's cells).

Of particular importance is human neural development in its early stages. There is a large body of research investigating the role of DHA in the development of the brain and nervous system in fetuses and young infants. The fact that DHA is specifically incorporated into the membrane phospholipids of the brain and retina, and that it is the "preferred" essential fatty acid for these tissues is not disputed. In fact, so prevalent is DHA in the makeup of the brain and retina that researchers and health experts are beginning once again to emphasize how important this fatty acid can be.

Joyce Nettleton, author of Omega-3 Fatty Acids and Health, states that although existing data can be criticized for not being definitive or failing to demonstrate deficiency symptoms unequivocally, researchers active in this area are taking the position that omega-3 fatty acids (DHAS) are essential for the optimum fetal development of neural tissues (Nettleton 253-55). Nettleton reviews the research literature concerning early brain development, noting that DHA is the preferred and most necessary acid. She also notes that it is important to consistently consume DHA: trial animals fed a DHA-deficient diet for three weeks lost half of their brain DHA; animals fed any source of omega-3 acids experienced increased levels of brain DHA, and those fed specifically DHA instead of LNA accumulated nearly four times the amount. (Nettleton 254).

Other researchers affirm Nettleton's claims. The authors of a recent study investigating the role of DHA in early neural development say that the presence of DHA and other fatty acids is "extremely important " during early development and that failing to maintain intake of these fatty acids (which would be found in human milk) could cause "permanent adverse effects" (Farquarson et al 810-813). What these researchers say only reiterates the importance of ensuring that developing fetuses receive the adequate levels of DHA during at least the latter stages of pregnancy, and that these same fetuses continue adequate intake of DHA, most notably through the mother's milk.

Another recent study provides additional valuable insight into the importance of DHA consumption during early human development, particularly in the area of brain and nervous system function. The study notes that a total of 135 breastfed and 391 formula-fed children were given a follow-up neurological after nine years. Children fed with formula milk or formula supplemented with breast milk within the first three weeks of life were found to have twice the rate of minor neurological dysfunction as compared to children fully breastfed for at least the first 21 days of life. The authors then note that one of the probable reasons for the results was the "beneficial effects of essential long chain fatty acids (arachidonic, docosahexaenic [DHA]) known to be present in breast milk and missing in most infant formulas. These essential fatty acids are needed for the structural development of brain and neural tissue" (Lanting 1319-1322).

Importance of DHA during Pregnancy and Nursing

We know that an infant's brain is most able to utilize DHA during the last trimester of pregnancy and the first few months of life; this brings up the question of how and when an infant best receives DHA. For years, the argument of which is better—breastfeeding or formula feeding—has raged on. Certainly, formula provides basic nutrients and is better that giving cow's milk, juice or other products that may be hard to digest or depleted of worthwhile ingredients. But recent research indicates that a mother's milk is the best (and probably only) way for an infant to receive adequate levels of DHA.

Results of various studies show that it is extremely important for a developing baby (both in the womb and in infancy) to have adequate levels of DHA for optimal mental and vision function. Though not completely researched, data does indicate that the mental and visual capabilities of infants provided DHA-deficient diets, on average, suffer from a variety of conditions, including impaired learning, lower IQ scores, and vision disorders. Simply put, researchers of one study investigating the role of DHA and other omega-3s in early human development state, " The higher concentration of DHA in brains of breast-fed infants may explain the improved neuro-development reported in breast-fed compared with formula-fed infants (Makrides et al 189-94).

Breast Feeding vs. Formula Feeding

A 1992 study investigating the polyunsaturated fatty acid (PUFA) compositions of breast milk and infant formula supports the notion that a mother's milk is the optimal source for DHA. Of the twenty term and two preterm infants studied, one of the preterm infants, fed formula only, had the lowest DHA levels. Lucas and colleagues concluded in this 1992 study that breast milk contains many aspects, possibly long chain PUFAs (like DHA, EPA, and AA), not found in proprietary infant formulae that are beneficial to infant neurodevelopment. Lack of dietary omega-3 fatty acids reduces the DHA content of rat brain and may impair rats' learning ability. The structure and function of cortical membrane phospholipids is likely to be extremely important during early development and failure to maintain an intake of fatty acids similar to that provided by mature human milk may cause permanent adverse effects.

The authors also go on to make a recommendation concerning the inclusion of DHA in infant formula: "At least trace quantities of DHA should be included in artificial formulae intended for all infants; and formulae designed specifically for preterm infants should contain both DHA and AA" (Farquarson et al 812-813).

A 1994 study supports the previous claims. This study involved 35 term infants, 15 of which were breastfed and 20 of which were formula fed. The study's authors note that human milk does supply the full range of PUFAs, saying "Human milk provides infants with a full complement of all PUFAs, including DHA and arachidonic acid (AA). Formula only contains the precursors alpha linolenic acid (ALA) and linoleic acid (LA), and hence, formula-fed infants must synthesize their own DHA and AA" (Makrides et al 189).The authors also note that: "[b]reast-fed infants score better on visual and developmental tests than do formula-fed infants, and this has been related to higher concentrations of erythrocyte [red blood cell] DHA. .Breast-fed infants [in this study] had a greater proportion of DHA in their erythrocytes and brain cortex relative to those fed formula. . .Cortex DHA increased in breast-fed (but not formula-fed) infants with age, largely an effect of length of feeding" (189). Developing brain tissue benefits more from the essential amino chains in human milk, than with the baby formula, but what can be done to slow the aging process in the maturing brain?

Alpha Lipoic Acid and the Aging Process

Frequently the oxidative stress caused by free radicals, as discussed above, results in what we refer to as the "aging process." While aging is inevitable, many of us hasten its outcome by not protecting ourselves, and thus, we age prematurely. The early onset of wrinkling, arthritis, circulatory disorders, diabetes, heart disease, and hardening of the arteries, as well as brain tissue damage, can result from free-radical destruction that could have been minimized by consistently taking strong antioxidants. Brain function is also affected by the aging process.

Dr. Richard Passwater, author of Cancer Prevention and Nutritional Therapies states, "They [antioxidants] may be much more important than doctors thought in warding off cancer, heart disease and the ravages of aging—and no, you may not be getting enough of these nutrients in your diet" (85).

Levels of ALA, like supplies of human growth hormone, DHEA, melatonin; and coenzyme Q10, decrease with age (Packer 227-230). This happens because the body's ability to synthesize these compounds declines, therefore food sources that contain Because the lack of every one of these compounds has been associated with the aging process, ALA becomes even more important.

This implies that if we could replace levels of ALA and other biochemicals before aging occurs, the process could be significantly inhibited. In addition, Dr. Packer points out that because we are living longer and are exposed to harmful chemicals more often, we have to deal with increased incidence of age-related diseases.

BRAIN TISSUE PROTECTION

Researchers at the University of Rochester Medical Center found that ALA protected brain cells from certain hazardous chemicals. One of these was N-methyl-daspartate (or NMDA) which, when administered in excess, can cause neuron damage in the nervous system. Researchers involved in these trials reported that ALA may play a possible role in the treatment of acute or chronic neurological disorders such as Huntington's disease. It stands to reason that other neurological disorders may respond to ALA therapy, and while research with other diseases is lacking, supplementation may benefit anyone who suffers from Parkinson's disease, multiple sclerosis, and related disorders.

Alzheimer's Disease

One of the most promising properties of ALA is the fact that it can protect brain tissue on a cellular level. Studies have been done not only on how ALA helps with neurological disorders resulting from external exposure, but also disorders such as memory loss that could be the result of normal processes like oxidation. German animal studies have found that ALA supplementation caused no difference in young mice, but a big improvement in the long-term memory of aged mice. What this finding implies is that ALA must help to reverse age-related memory impairment. by protecting brain cells from the kind of deterioration brought on by oxidation over time. Researchers believe that the chemical compounds found in ALA may help to treat a number of age-related neurological disorders like Alzheimer's disease.

Stroke

Because ALA goes into brain tissue, it can help to prevent the type of cellular damage which usually occurs when a portion of the brain becomes oxygen starved. Dr. Packer's research also found that ALA can significantly increase the rate of survival in rats that had suffered a stroke if administered prior to the stroke. In a study, blood flow to the brains of test rats was restricted for 30 minutes, after which it was restored. Within 24 hours, 80 percent of the rats died. If they received lipoic acid, only 20 percent died—a result he refers to as the "most remarkable effect I've ever found in cerebral ischemia in a model system" (Interview—Packer Health World). One of the main causes of death was the dramatic dropping of glutathione levels when blood flow was stopped to brain tissue. Even the administration of glutathione did not remedy this deficit. It was through ALA supplementation that glutathione levels increased, lowering the mortality rate.

The Healing Power of Herbs

The natural herbs Ginseng and Ginkgo biloba have both been used for thousands of years in traditional Chinese medicine because of their effect on the brain and overall well-being. In recent times, they have become popular for their medicinal uses and research is now being done to scientifically determine the assets of both herbs as supplements for memory and stress reduction. Another agent which began its use in China centuries ago, Huperzine A has been shown to exhibit memory enhancement and other positive effects in the brain.

HUPERZINE A AND MEMORY

Huperzine A, (HUPA) a novel alkaloid isolated from the Chinese herb Huperzia serrata, has been used for centuries in China to treat fever and inflammation. HUPA is a potent and selective inhibitor of acetylcholinerase (AChE) and is rapidly absorbed into the brain in experimental animals. Huperzine A exhibits memory enhancing activities in a broad range of cognitive processes. Huperzine is suggested by researchers to be a "promising candidate for clinical development as a symptomatic treatment for Alzheimer's disease" (Tang 481-84).

Research demonstrates that HUPA exerts beneficial effects on memory deficits. In a multicenter, double-blind placebo controlled study, 50 patients were administered orally 4 tablets HUPA and 53 patients were given 4 tablets of placebo for 8 weeks. Patients were examined for memory, dementia, mental health, and activity of daily living scale. About 58 percent of patients treated with HUPA showed improvement in their memory, cognitive, and behavioral functions. The efficacy of HUPA was better than placebo. And no severe side effect was found. This study also supports that HUPA is a promising potential therapy for Alzheimer's disease (Xu 391-5).

Huperzine's ability to prevent seizures and subsequent

neuropathological changes has also been studied. In a study conducted on pigs, HUPA, given before seizures, protected against soman-induced convulsions and neuropathological changes in the hippo campus. This activity seems to be related to a protection by HUPA of stores of AChE. (Lallement 387-90). Further data suggest that HUPA could be a potent neuroprotective agent where neurons are impaired and other function is compromised (Ved 963-66).

GINSENG—THE STRESS REDUCER

Siberian ginseng is a shrub which grows in parts of the Soviet far East, Korea, China, and Japan. The root and leaves are both used medicinally. The use of ginseng in Chinese herbal medicine dates back more than 4,000 years. The Chinese believe that regular use of Siberian ginseng will increase longevity, improve general health, improve the appetite and restore memory.

Ginseng root has since been found to improve brain function and memory, stimulate the action of the endocrine glands and strengthen the central nervous system. A study from the late 1950s performed by Russian scientist Brekhov suggested that ginseng improved reading capacity of subjects. During the test, reading ability improved after subjects took ginseng, and the improvements continued for up to six weeks after the test. (Krochmal 1978). An Asian confirmed that ginseng improved brain function in a different way: radio operators were given either ginseng extract or a placebo; those given the ginseng made fewer mistakes in their communications. The ginseng helped to increase stamina and improve brain function (Foster 4). Daniel Mowrey also notes that Siberian ginseng has been found to help improve mental abilities in geriatric patients (Mowrey 192).

Besides improving brain function as noted above, ginseng works as an adaptogen to reduce stress. Ginseng helps to modify the effects of both environmental and internal stress, which causes a disturbance in the body physically and/or mentally. This stress can come from different origins such as chemical pollutants, toxins, radiation, physical trauma, and emotional stress. Because of its adaptogenic properties, ginseng is able to adjust and balance the body functions when they are under stress. (Mills 531). Michael Murray, N.D. explains that ginseng can do this by helping to balance the hypothalamic-pituitary-adrenal axis through the normalization of the metabolic systems in the body when stress occurs (Murray 127).

Farnsworth and colleagues have reviewed data on a Ginseng root extract that has been administered to more that 2,100 healthy human subjects in clinical trials for the purpose of evaluating the adaptogenic effects of Siberian ginseng (156-215). These studies indicate that Siberian ginseng (1) increased the ability of humans to withstand many adverse physical conditions i.e., heat, noise, motion, work load increase, exercise, and decompression, (2) increased mental alertness and work output, and (3) improved the quality of work produced under stressful conditions. The studies included both male and female subjects ranging in age from 19 to 72 years.

Siberian ginseng shows adaptogenic activity in diseases affecting the brain as well. It has consistently demonstrated an ability to increase sense of well-being regardless of the psychological complaint (insomnia, hypochondriasis, various neuroses, etc.) A possible explanation for this effect is an improvement in balance between the various biogenic amines (serotonin, dopamine, norepinephrine, etc.), which act as transmitters in the nervous system, as Siberian ginseng extract administered to rats has been shown to increase biogenic amine content in the brain, adrenals, and urine.

Ginseng and Chronic Fatigue Syndrome

One of the more popular uses of Siberian ginseng is in the treatment of "Chronic Fatigue Syndrome" (CFS). Although a newly defined illness, CFS has been around a long time. Chronic fatigue syndrome can be a debilitating illness characterized by persistent fatigue along with other symptoms including low-grade fever, frequent sore throats, joint and muscle pain, and various neuro/psychological symptoms such as depression. Central to CFS is a disturbed immune system. While research has focused on trying to identify a specific infectious organism, CFS is more likely due to a general immune system failure. Effective treatment of CFS must be comprehensive and address underlying factors that contribute to the weakened status of the immune system. However, Siberian ginseng appears to address the fatigue, decreased sense of well-being, and impaired immune functions.

Siberian ginseng has been shown to exert a number of beneficial effects that may be useful in the treatment of CFS. In one double-blind study, thirty-six healthy subjects received either 10 ml of a Siberian ginseng extract or placebo daily for 4 weeks.(Bohn et al 1193-1196) The group receiving the Siberian ginseng fluid extract demonstrated significant improvement in a variety of immune system parameters. Most notable were a significant increase in helper T cells and an increase in natural killer cell activity. Both of these effects could be put to good use in the treatment of chronic fatigue system.

GINKGO BILOBA

Ginkgo biloba extract (GBE) is a popular herb used to enhance mental clarity and circulation in the brain and extremities. It exerts a profound, widespread influence on tissue, including membrane-stabilizing, antioxidant, and free radical-scavenging effects. GBE also enhances the utilization of oxygen and glucose.

Cellular membranes provide the first line of defense in maintaining the integrity of the cell. Largely composed of fatty acids, cellular membranes also serve as fluid barriers, exchange sites, and electrical capacitors. These membranes are fragile and vulnerable to damage, especially the lipid peroxidation induced by oxygenated free radicals. GBE is an extremely effective inhibitor of lipid peroxidation of cellular membranes.

Red blood cells provide excellent models for evaluating the effects of substances on membrane function. Red blood cell studies utilizing GBE have demonstrated that in addition to directly stabilizing membrane structures and scavenging free radicals, GBE also enhances membrane transport of potassium into (and sodium out of) the cell by activating the sodium pump. In essence, GBE leads to better polarization. This is particularly important in excitable tissues, such as nerve cells.

The membrane-stabilizing and free-radical scavenging effects of GBE are perhaps most evident in the brain and nerve cells. Brain cells contain the highest percentage of unsaturated fatty acids in the membranes of any cells in the body, making them extremely susceptible to free radical damage. The brain cell is also extremely susceptible to hypoxia. Unlike most other tissues, the brain has very little energy reserve. Its function requires large amounts of energy in the form of a constant supply of glucose and oxygen. Diminished circulation to the brain sets of a chain of reactions that disrupt membrane function and energy production and ultimately lead to cellular death.

Ginkgo and Mental Clarity

Ginkgo biloba extract shows great benefit in many cases of senility, including Alzheimer's disease. In addition to GBE's ability to increase the functional capacity of the brain via the mechanisms described above, it has also been shown to normalize the acetylcholine receptors in the hippo campus of aged animals, to increase cholinergic transmission, and to address many of the other major elements of Alzheimer's disease. Although preliminary studies in established Alzheimer's patients are quite promising, it appears at this time that GBE is most effective in delaying mental deterioration in the early stages of Alzheimer's disease. If mental deficit is due to vascular insufficiency or depression and not Alzheimer's disease, GBE is usually effective in reversing the deficit.

Ginkgo biloba has been recommended for problems related to memory loss and retention typically found in the elderly. In one study, 156 patients with degenerative dementia of Alzheimer's type and multi-infarct dementia were give GBE in a prospective, randomized, double-blind, placebo-controlled study over a 24 week period. Psycho pathological assessment, attention, memory, and behavioral assessment of daily activities were studied. The frequency of therapy responders in the two treatment groups differed significantly in favor of the GBE group. This well-designed study demonstrated the clinical efficacy of GBE for Alzheimer's type dementia. Although increased brain activity was seen after a single dose, the most dramatic changes did not appear for six months.

A recent review surveyed the quality of research in more that forty clinical studies on GBE in the treatment of cerebral insufficiency. The results of the analysis indicate that GBE is effective in reducing all symptoms of cerebral insufficiency, including impaired mental function (senility), and the quality of performance was comparable to Hydergine, an FDA-approved drug used in the treatment of cerebral vascular insufficiency and Alzheimer's disease. It appears that by increasing cerebral blood flow and therefore oxygen and glucose utilization, GBE offers relief of these presumed "side effects" of aging and may offer significant protection against their development.

Circulation in the Brain

GBE is remarkable for its ability to prevent metabolic disturbances in experimental models of insufficient blood supply to the brain. It accomplishes this by enhancing oxygen utilization and increasing cellular uptake of glucose, thus restoring energy production. Briefly, GBE promotes an increased nerve transmission rate, improves synthesis and turnover of brain neurotransmitters and normalizes acetylcholine receptors in the hippo campus (the area of the brain most affected by Alzheimer's disease).

In general, GBE exerts its vascular effects primarily on the lining of the blood vessels and the system that regulates blood vessel tone. GBE stimulates greater tone in the venous system, thus aiding the dynamic clearing of toxic metabolites that accumulate during times of insufficient blood supply. *Ginkgo biloba* extract's primary clinical application has been in the treatment of vascular insufficiency or insufficient blood flow to the brain in more than fifty double-blind clinical trials of patients with chronic cerebral (brain) arterial insufficiency and patients with peripheral arterial insufficiency and mental performance. These symptoms include short-term memory loss, vertigo, headache, ringing in the ears, and depression. The significant regression of these symptoms following treatment with GBE suggests that vascular insufficiency may be the major causative factor accounting for these so-called "age-related cerebral disorders," rather that a true degenerative process.

As well as improving blood supply to the brain, experimental and clinical studies show that GBE increases the rate at which information is transmitted at the nerve cell level. The memory enhancing effects of GBE are not limited to the elderly. In one double-blind study, the reaction time in healthy young women performing a memory test improved significantly after the administration of GBE.

Neurological Diseases

PARKINSON'S DISEASE

Parkinson's disease is a degenerative disease of the nervous system. Approximately one person in two hundred is affected by this disease with 50,000 new cases diagnosed in the US each year. Elderly people are the most vulnerable to Parkinson's disease and men are more likely to be affected than women. The disease usually begins between the ages of 50 and 65. Untreated, Parkinson's disease can progress over ten to fifteen years, resulting in severe incapacity. With modern drug treatment and natural supplementation, the outlook is significantly more positive.

The disease will usually begin with a slight tremor of one hand, arm or leg. In this stage, the tremor is worse when the hand or limb is at rest. As the disease progresses, both sides of the body will be affected causing weakness, stiffness, an unsure shuffling walk, head shaking, drooling, unblinking gaze, and a gradual inability to take care of everyday demands. When the disease is in the latter stages, intellect may become affected. During this stage, speech may be slow and handwriting may be illegible. Depression is also commonly apparent in victims of Parkinson's disease.

Causes

The specific cause of this disease is well known. It is caused by an imbalance of dopamine and acetylcholine, two chemicals found in the brain. A deficiency of dopamine in certain brain cells inhibits brain messages transmitted from one cell to another. As a result, a degeneration of these nerve cell clusters occurs. This degeneration of nerve cells in the brain affects the way muscle tension and movement is controlled, causing the muscles to remain overly tense.

Other factors which have been linked to the disease are viral infections, heavy metal exposure, faulty mineral metabolism, aluminum ingestion, and manganese, mercury and carbon monoxide poisoning. Parkinson's disease can also be the result of an earlier brain infection such as encephalitis. There is some evidence that the disease is hereditary. Certain nutritional supplements have been recommended in Parkinson's disease therapy.

Recommended Nutritional Supplements

Alpha lipoic acid: This antioxidant discussed earlier, facilitates the action of vitamins E and C, which are both excellent free radical scavengers in the brain. Researchers at the University of Rochester Medical Center found that ALA protected brain cells from certain hazardous chemicals which have been associated with Parkinson's disease.

Essential Fatty Acids: Because the brain is primarily composed of unsaturated fatty acids, supplying the right kind of fatty acid compounds in diseases like Parkinson's is vital. Canadian researchers have used evening primrose oil as a clinical treatment for Parkinson's and other tremor causing diseases (Critchley 207).

Ginkgo biloba: This supplement works to boost brain cell oxygenation which can help inhibit the progression of senile dementia (Allain et al 54-58).

Niacin: Nicotinic acid can actually prolong elevated levels of brain dopa and dopamine in patients who were taking L-dopa as a treatment for Parkinson's (Block 244-251).

ALZHEIMER'S DISEASE

Alzheimer's disease is a progressive, degenerative condition that involves the deterioration of nerve cells in the brain, resulting in memory loss and disorientation. The disease is thought to be responsible for seventy-five percent of dementia in those 65 years and older.

Unfortunately, the intellectual and personal decline that typically results from Alzheimer's cannot be curtailed as of yet. The disease affects over 4 million Americans and is responsible for twenty percent of patients in nursing homes or chronic care facilities. The disease rarely manifests itself before age 60. Up to thirty percent of people over 85 suffer from Alzheimer's.

There are three general stages to the disease. Initial symptoms include increasing forgetfulness, which may be addressed by the almost obsessive writing of lists. As the disease progresses, forgetfulness becomes severe memory loss, particularly when dealing with short term events even though long-term memory may not be affected. Disorientation may also occur and it is not uncommon for a victim of the disease to lose his way home. Mathematical calculations may also become difficult, indicating a decrease in intellectual ability in addition to becoming unable to find the right words. Anxiety, mood swings, and apprehension may become apparent and personality changes can also be evident.

During the final stage of Alzheimer's, severe disorientation and confusion are the rule as are hallucinations and paranoid delusions. These symptoms typically intensify at night. In addition, involuntary actions, urinary and feces incontinence, and belligerence and violent behavior are not uncommon, although some victims become more docile and withdrawn. Tendency of Alzheimer's sufferers to wander and neglect their appearance and hygiene often necessitates confinement to a bed. Once exiled, their life expectancy decreases.

However, many older people with a number of psychological symptoms ranging from depression to dementia, can mistake malnutrition for Alzheimer's disease. Consequently, it is important that diet be assessed and that vitamin and mineral supplements be added to determine if nutritional depletion is the cause. The B vitamins are particularly vital. In addition, certain drugs can cause memory deficit or altered psychological behavior.

Causes

The causes are Alzheimer's remain unknown although several theories exist which range from blaming aluminum exposure to the existence of prolonged infection. Another possible cause, reduced levels of acetylcholine (a brain chemical)in the brain, has been found in people suffering from the disease. Deficiencies like vitamin B12, zinc, potassium, selenium, and boron were also found. Also, there is evidence that increased contact with aluminum in combination with a lack of certain vitamins and minerals may predispose a person to the disease.

Recommended Nutritional Supplements

Alpha Lipoic Acid: German Studies have found that ALA supplementation caused an improvement in the long-term memory of aged mice, while younger mice showed no difference. This finding implies that ALA must help to reverse the age-related memory impairment.

Ginkgo biloba: Clinical studies are supportive of this herb's ability to reverse the mental deterioration associated with early stages of Alzheimer's disease (Hofferberth page). It improves brain cell oxygenation and circulation and is highly recommended. Ginkgo is good for treating the early symptoms of Alzheimer's.

Phosphatidyl Choline: Increases acetylcholine levels in

the brain which directly impacts memory function. Clinical data suggests that elevating acetylcholine in the brain may improve memory in Alzheimer's patients (Canty 327-39).

Phosphatidyl Serine: This compound is one of the primary phospholipids found in brain tissue and plays an important role in brain function. Animal and human studies have found that supplementing this nutrient can improve memory and age-related changes in brain chemistr (Crook et al 61-66).

Vitamin E: Helps transport oxygen to brain cells and scavenges for free radicals which can cause brain tissue damage. Vitamin E has been shown to help stabilize the symptoms of the disease and retard its progression.

Conclusion

Familiarity with some of the potential damage and change your brain can go through during the natural aging process will help you make an informed decision about what you can do to enjoy optimal brain activity. Supplementing a healthy diet with the necessary antioxidants, essential fatty acids, herbs, and the other compounds mentioned can give you more brain power as well as protect against potential damage and deterioration. Because these agents have the ability to increase brain productivity, mental clarity and your general sense of well-being.

More information about the brain, the diseases that can affect it, and possible treatment and prevention can be found in Dr. Paul Barney's *Doctor's Guide to Natural Medicine* (see bibliography).

Works Cited

Allain, H. et al. "Effect of two doses of ginkgo biloba extract on the dual coding test in elderly subjects," Clinical Therapy, 1993, 15(3): 54-58.

Block, M. and R Brandft.. "Nicotinic acid or N-methyl nicotinamide prolongs elevated brain dopa amd dopamine in L-dopa treatment," Biochem Med Metab Biol, 1986, 36(2): 244-51.

Canty, D.J. and S.H. Zeisel. "Lecithin and Choline in human health disease. " Nutr Reviews, 19994, 52: 327-339.

Critchley, E. "Evening Primrose Oil (Efamol) in Parkinsonian and other tremors; as a preliminary study" In D.F. Horrobin, ed. Clinical Uses of Essential Fatty Acids, (Eden Press, Montreal: 1982), 205-08.

Crook, T. et al. "Effects of phosphatidyl in Alzheimer's disease," Psychopharmacology Bulletin, 1992, 28: 61-66.

Farquarson, James et al. "Infant Cerebral Cortex Phospholipid Fatty-Acid Composition and Diet." Lancet 340 (October 1992): 810-813.

Foster, Steven. Asian Ginseng Botanical Series No 303, 1991, 4.

Gutteridge, John M.C. and Barry Halliwell. Antioxidants in Nutrition, Health and Disease. (Oxford: Oxford University Press, 1994), 7, 53.

Hofferberth, B. The Efficacy of Egb761 in patients with senile dementia of the Alzheimer's type: A double-blind, placebo-controlled study on different levels of investigation," Human Psycho pharmacology

Krochmal, Arnold and Connie. Garden Magazine, Sept-Oct. 1978

Lallement, G. et al. Efficacy of huperzine in preventing soman-induced seizures, neuropathological changes, and lethality. Fundamental Clinical Pharmacology 1997; 11(5):387-4.

Lanting, C.I. "Neurological differences between 9 year-old children fed breast-milk or formula as babies." Lancet 344 (1994): 1319-1322.

Lieberman, Sheri, Ph.D. and Nancy Bruning, The Real Vitamin and Mineral Book. (New York: Avery Publishing Group, 1997), 6.

Lin, David J. Free Radicals and Disease Prevention: What You Must Know. (New Canaan, CT: Keats Publishing, Inc., 1993), 11.

Makrides, Maria et al. "Fatty Acid Composition of Brain, Retina, and Ethrocytes in Breast- and Formula-Fed Infants." American Journal of Clinical Nutrition 60 (1994): 189-94.

Mills, Simon Y. The Essential Book of Herbal Medicine. London: Penguin Books, 1993, 531.

Mowrey, Daniel B., Ph.D. The Scientific Validation of Herbs, (New Canaan, CT: Keats Publishing. Inc. 1986,)192.

Murray, Michael T., N.D. Male Sexual Vitality, Rocklin, CA: Prima Publishing, 1991), 127.

Nettleton, Joyce. Omega-3 Fatty Acids, New York,: Chapman and Hall, 1995, 253-55.

Neuringer, M. et al. "Dietary Omega-3 Fatty Acid Deficiency and Visual Loss in Infant Rhesus Monkeys" Journal of Clinical Investigation, 73 (1984): 272-76.

Packer Health World http://www.healthworld.com/ LIBRARY/ARTICLE/PASSWATER/PACKER3.HTM

Packer, Lester, PhD et al. "Alpha lipoic acid as a biological antioxidant," Free Radical Biology and Medicine, 1995 19: 227-250.

Passwater, Richard A. Cancer Prevention and Nutritional Therapies, (new Canaan, Connecticut: Keats Publishing, 1993; 85.

Sano, Mary et al. "A Controlled Trial of Selegeline, Alpha-Tocopherol, or Both as a Treatment for Alzheimer's Disease," New England Journal of Medicine, 336 (1997): 1216-1222.

Tang XC. Huperzine A: A promising drug for Alzheimer's disease. Chung Kuo Yao Li Hsuch Pao 1996 Nov., 17(6):481-84.

Xu SS et al. Chung Kuo Yao Li Hsueh Pao 1995 Sept. 16(5):391-5.